IQ WORKOUT

BULLET GUIDE

Mac Bride

Hodder Education, 338 Euston Road, London NW1 3BH

Hodder Education is an Hachette UK company

First published in UK 2012 by Hodder Education

This edition published 2012

Copyright © 2012 Mac Bride

The moral rights of the author have been asserted.

Database right Hodder Education (makers)

Artworks (internal and cover): Peter Lubach
Cover concept design: Two Associates

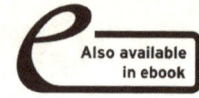

Also available
in ebook

All rights reserved. No part of this publication may be reproduced, stored in a retrieval system or transmitted in any form or by any means, electronic, mechanical, photocopying, recording or otherwise, without the prior permission in writing of Hodder Education, or as expressly permitted by law, or under terms agreed with the appropriate reprographic rights organization. Enquiries concerning reproduction outside the scope of the above should be sent to the Rights Department, Hodder Education, at the address above.

You must not circulate this book in any other binding or cover and you must impose this same condition on any acquirer.

British Library Cataloguing in Publication Data: a catalogue record for this title is available from the British Library.

10 9 8 7 6 5 4 3 2 1

The publisher has used its best endeavours to ensure that any website addresses referred to in this book are correct and active at the time of going to press. However, the publisher and the author have no responsibility for the websites and can make no guarantee that a site will remain live or that the content will remain relevant, decent or appropriate.

The publisher has made every effort to mark as such all words which it believes to be trademarks. The publisher should also like to make it clear that the presence of a word in the book, whether marked or unmarked, in no way affects its legal status as a trademark.

Every reasonable effort has been made by the publisher to trace the copyright holders of material in this book. Any errors or omissions should be notified in writing to the publisher, who will endeavour to rectify the situation for any reprints and future editions.

Hachette UK's policy is to use papers that are natural, renewable and recyclable products and made from wood grown in sustainable forests. The logging and manufacturing processes are expected to conform to the environmental regulations of the country of origin.

www.hoddereducation.co.uk

Typeset by Stephen Rowling/Springworks

Printed in Spain

Contents

About the author

Mac Bride saw his first book published in 1982, and since then he has written something over 120 books on various aspects of programming, computer applications, the Internet, languages for people buying houses overseas, green issues and other topics. As well as writing, he has edited and typeset books on subjects ranging from marketing through feng shui to allotment gardening. Mac says it's been a privilege to be able to follow his interests across so many fields – and to make a living from it! Before he was allowed to work on this book, Mac was asked to take an IQ test. It proved negative.

Introduction

Your IQ – 'raw intelligence' – is largely determined by genetics and by nutrition and environment in your early years. It cannot be increased in adults. However, you can improve the ability to apply that intelligence in the real world, to solve problems and to see connections.

This is largely a book to 'do' rather than to read. The first two chapters cover the theory, such as it is. We start with an introduction to the concept of intelligence – what it is and what the book aims to do, followed by a chapter on body and brain, because the physical health of the brain is a factor in its efficient functioning. The next six chapters contain puzzles and challenges designed to exercise different types of intelligence, with an introduction to the techniques for tackling them. Chapter 9 is also to be used actively. It teaches some simple but effective techniques for improving your memory – another important aspect of increasing the 'brain power'. The final chapter gives the answers to the puzzles, with notes where appropriate.

Take your time working through this book, and enjoy the process.

1 Intelligence and IQ

IQ workout?

What is an **IQ workout**? That should be the first question you ask yourself after seeing this title. And 'Will it leave my brain hot and sweaty, but better for the exercise?' might well be the next. I'll try to answer the first question in this chapter, and I hope that you will have an answer to the second after you have tackled some of the stuff in this book.

Will an IQ workout leave my brain hot and sweaty?
· ·

But the immediate questions are:

* What does **IQ** stand for?
* What does it measure? (The answer is not as obvious as it may appear.)
* What is **intelligence**? (Ditto)
* Can you increase your IQ?

The answers to these are in the next few pages.

Test your IQ online

If you'd like to know your IQ, there are many free (and paid for) tests available online. Don't take the results too seriously – they are not that accurate, and different test will give different results. Use only tests based in your country – a Brit will score lower on a US-based test than on one designed in the UK. (See pages 8–9 for the reasons why.) Search online for 'IQ tests' to get started.

What is intelligence?

Intelligence is hard to define exactly, but can probably be best thought of as the ability to:

* learn new things
* understand ideas
* solve problems.

Fluid and crystallized intelligence

Psychologists identify two types of intelligence:

* **Fluid intelligence** Reasoning and problem solving ability, typically measured by visual and logical tests.
* **Crystallized intelligence** The ability to apply learned skills and knowledge, which can be measured by testing vocabulary, maths, etc.

The two combine to make your overall intelligence. But notice that neither can be measured by any single test – intelligence is too complex for that.

What else affects brain power?

Mental performance doesn't just depend upon intelligence. Other factors are also important. These include:

* **Processing speed** How quickly you can think, and maintain full attention.
* **Reaction time** How quickly you can react to a stimulus.
* **Short-term memory** The ability to take in information and use it within a few seconds.
* **Long-term memory** The ability to store information and retrieve it later, as needed.

**If the human brain were so simple
that we could understand it,
we would be so simple that we couldn't.**

Emerson M. Pugh

IQ tests

IQ stands for **intelligence quotient** and an IQ test is supposed to measure intelligence, but, as intelligence isn't a simple quality, there is no simple way to measure it.

IQ tests normally have a battery of questions of different sorts to measure:

* verbal ability
* mathematical ability
* logical reasoning
* visual–spatial ability.

IQ tests are **standardized**, but, as different ones set different questions in different quantities, a person's score will vary depending upon the test. And practice at IQ tests improves your score. The result you get from any IQ test is never anything more than an approximate measure of some types of intellectual ability.

The IQ bell curve

If you plot the IQ scores of a population on a graph, you get a 'bell-shaped' curve. Scores are standardized to give an average score of 100, with a matching spread on either side. Two-thirds of the results fall within 15 points of the average (85 to 115), and 95% fall between 70 and 130. Very few are at either end of the scale – only 1 in 1000 score under 55 or over 145 points.

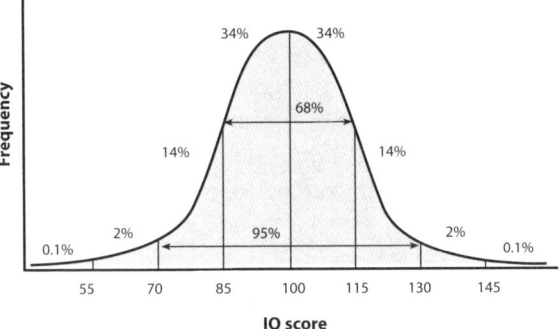

What an IQ test measures best is your ability to do IQ tests

Some facts about IQ tests

* IQ tests assess only four types of brain activity – verbal and numeric ability, spatial perception and processing speed.
* People who score highly on one part of an IQ test will generally score highly on the others.
* People's overall scores in different IQ tests vary but are more consistent at the top and bottom end of the scales.
* IQ tests are never culture-free. They will always, to a greater or lesser extent, reflect the language, education and customs of the time and place in which they are based.

* The average IQ score tends to be lower in older age groups. This is probably due to the changing cultural and educational environment that people grow up in.
* Genes are more important than environment. Twins tend to get very similar scores whether they are raised together or in different homes. But there is no correlation between racial origins and intelligence.
* Practice and training can improve IQ scores.
* IQ tests do not assess creativity, common sense, social sensitivity, kindness, charisma or many other aspects of personality.

I took an IQ test and the results were negative

Intelligence and age

Your level of raw intelligence stops increasing in your teens – just as you stop growing taller – and you can't change this any more than you can grow taller. However, you can learn to make better use of your brain so that you can:

* learn new things faster
* understand more complex ideas
* solve more difficult problems, faster.

But there's a downside. If the brain doesn't get enough stimulation, it will start to deteriorate. Use it or lose it!

You can learn to make better use of your brain

What can make you smarter?

There is a positive link between **musical training** in childhood and higher IQ. This may mean that the training improves children's IQ, or it may reflect the nature of the parents who encourage children to take up an instrument.

Training the 'working' (short-term) memory may increase the IQ. Recent research shows that it does improve performance on some parts of the IQ tests, but it's not clear how far it extends to other aspects of fluid intelligence. What is self-evident is that memory training will improve overall mental performance, whether it affects the IQ score or not.

Social interaction and **mental stimulation** both help to stave off mental decline with age. When you retire, take up bridge and ballroom dancing if you want to stay young (see page 22).

2 Brain chemistry

Healthy body, healthy mind

The simple fact is, your brain works better if your body is in good shape. Your brain is part of your body and can't do its job properly if it's low on oxygen or has the wrong hormones and other chemicals washing through it.

Your intellectual performance is also affected by your emotional state and by social activity (really!). Stress, depression, negative emotions and social isolation all tend to impair mental functioning.

A regular workout for your body is part of the workout for your IQ.

Your brain works better if your body is in good shape

Brain health checklist

- ☐ Do you eat the right sorts and avoid the wrong sorts of foods?
- ☐ Do you drink too much alcohol?
- ☐ Do you take enough exercise?
- ☐ Do you get enough sleep?
- ☐ Are you socially active, interacting with others regularly?

What's enough? What's right and wrong? What's too much? Read on …

If stress is a problem, the *Beat Stress Bullet Guide* may help.

What's in your head?

The human brain contains more than 100 billion **neurons** (nerve cells). These can collect and transmit electrochemical signals, as the components of a computer chip do with electromagnetic signals. Each cell has a single **axon**, which carries the electrical signals, and any number of tinier **dendrites,** which receive the signals. One neuron can link to thousands of others, creating literally trillions of **synapses** (connections). By the time a child's brain is fully developed physically – at about age 3 – it will have around 1,000,000,000,000,000 synapses. We lose them as we age, but a mature adult will still have getting on for half of them left, and 500 trillion synapses offers a lot of storage.

The brain is a wonderful organ. It starts working the moment you get up in the morning and does not stop until you get into the office.

Robert Frost

16

Some synapses are temporary – which is good if you are just thinking, but not so good if you need to retain a memory. They become permanent through repetition – either because of the intensity of the initial experience or by repeated exposure.

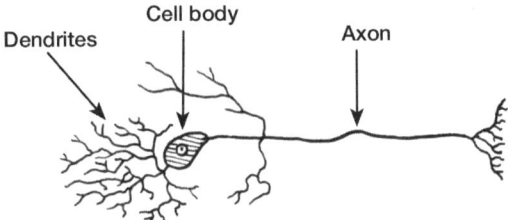

Cell body

Dendrites

Axon

● A neuron – there are about 100 billion of these in your head!

There's no evidence that you can run out of synapses, or that overuse can damage the brain, but there is clear evidence that lack of stimulation can reduce the brain's ability to make new connections.

Food for thought

Though the brain is a small fraction of your body weight, it uses about 20% of the total energy. To function well, the brain needs a good blood supply, which means well-oxygenated blood flowing freely through unclogged arteries. As well as sugar and oxygen, the brain needs:

✳ **Essential fatty acids** are used to build the neurons and the axons that link them. The body cannot manufacture these, so you must get them in your diet. There are two types:
   » Omega 3 fatty acids are found in green vegetables, oily fish, flax seeds and walnuts.
   » Omega 6 fatty acids are found in sunflower, corn and sesame oils.

* **Flavonoids** are used to create the chemicals needed when dendrites are connecting to axons to make new connections in the brain. Tea, blueberries, red wine and cocoa are all good sources of flavonoids.
* **Vitamins** E, C, B12 and folate all seem to encourage good long-term brain health.

To function well, the brain needs a good blood supply

Getting the balance right

If you are overweight, you are more likely to have high cholesterol levels and clogged arteries and are more likely to develop dementia in later life. Unfortunately, if you adopt a low-fat diet to avoid this problem, the lack of essential fatty acids also makes it more likely that you will develop dementia.

Exercise is good for you

And it's not just good for your heart. Research shows that cardiovascular exercise – the sort that gets your heart beating faster and your lungs working harder – can make your brain larger, mainly by increasing the number of blood vessels. A better blood supply will deliver more energy to the brain, allowing it to work better.

If you are stressed, exercise will help. It will clear from your body the adrenalin and other stress hormones that tend to block thought.

Sleep well

The simple fact is that your brain is not at its best if you don't get enough sleep. Of course, as you train your memory to be more reliable, you will worry less about forgetting stuff and sleep better!

How much exercise do I need?

For general good health, 30 minutes moderate exercise three times a week is the recommended minimum. Moderate exercise can be anything – walking, cycling, sport, even gardening or housework. What matters is that you put in enough effort to raise your heart rate to 50% to 80% of your maximum – and that you enjoy it so that you keep doing it.

You can calculate your maximum heart rate for exercising by subtracting your age from 220. If you are 50 years old, your maximum heart rate would be 220–50 = 170, and target heart rate at least 85 and up to 140.

● Tortoise: 'It's taking part that matters, not who wins.' Hare: 'If you say so.'

... and brains need exercise too!

Your brain needs exercise if it is to stay in good shape, just as much as your body does. There is clear evidence that the 'if you don't use it, you lose it' rule applies here, as it does to muscle tone and joint flexibility. This is true at any age, but increasingly so as you get older. A recent large-scale study in Chicago showed that older people who regularly read the newspaper, played chess or draughts or otherwise engaged their brains were 2.6 times less likely to develop Alzheimer's disease.

If you don't use it, you lose it

Social networks build neural networks

The same Chicago study also showed that people with a larger social network were also less likely to suffer mental decline. Simply talking to people is a good stimulant. Combine social interaction with intellectual activity and physical exercise … and you have the perfect brain exercise. Take up:

* dancing
* rambling
* tennis, bowls, golf
* bridge (but walk to the club)
* amateur theatre or music
* anything else that gets you moving and doing things with other people.

● Dancing alone is good exercise for the body; dancing with others is good exercise for the brain

3 Word power!

Verbal aptitude

Word power isn't just about the words that you know. Verbal aptitude tests assess how you can manipulate words in a variety of ways. You may be asked to find the odd one out, or another word of the same type, or one in a similar relationship. You need to think about:

* **Meanings** Some words have several meanings, and not all may be obvious, e.g. *fair* – impartial, blonde, good enough, fun fair – but also *to fair* – to smooth the junction between two surfaces.
* **Sounds** Words can sound the same but be spelt differently, e.g. rain, rein, reign, and some sets of letters can be pronounced several ways, e.g. 'ough' as in cough, plough, through, though, borough.

* **Patterns** Which letters are where in the words, and how do they relate to each other, e.g. clinic, madam, legal, rover – all start and end with the same letter.
* **Prefixes and suffixes** You may be able to combine the words with the same prefix, suffix or other word, e.g. winner, knife, board, bin – can all be prefixed by 'bread'.

Word power isn't just about the words that you know
. . . .

Tackle tests this way
1 Think about the meanings.
2 Say the words.
3 Look at the letters.
4 Try out possible combinations.

Verbal test 1: Analogies

Think about the relationship between the first pair of words. Are they synonyms (same meaning) or antonyms (opposites)? Is one a part of, used by, made by or a characteristic of the other?

1 Butterfly is to caterpillar as frog is to:
   (a) amphibian   (b) fish   (c) tadpole   (d) toad

2 Artist is to paint as author is to:
   (a) literature   (b) book   (c) writer   (d) words

3 Knee is to toe as elbow is to:
   (a) wrist   (b) finger   (c) arm   (d) shoulder

4 Coward is to bravery as cheat is to:
   (a) fraud   (b) diligence   (c) honesty   (d) heroism

5 Car is to garage as airplane is to:
   (a) sky   (b) travel   (c) airport   (d) hangar

6 Regret is to apology as guilt is to:
   (a) confession   (b) denial   (c) fear   (d) investigation

7 Flexible is to stiff as pragmatic is to:
   (a) industrious (b) idealistic   (c) practical   (d) adaptable

8 Circle is to circumference as rectangle is to:
   (a) diagonal   (b) area   (c) perimeter   (d) oblong

9 Audio is to hearing as tactile is to:
   (a) hold   (b) sound   (c) fingertips   (d) touch

10 Later is to alert as early is to:
   (a) relay   (b) asleep   (c) change   (d) adjust

Verbal test 2: Odd man out

Which word does not belong with the others?

1 (a) bus   (b) bicycle   (c) van   (d) lorry   (e) car

2 (a) doctor   (b) optician   (c) surgeon   (d) vet   (e) nurse

3 (a) gloves   (b) slippers   (c) sandals   (d) shoes   (e) socks

4 (a) tonne   (b) kilogram   (c) pound   (d) carat   (e) litre

5 (a) love   (b) hate   (c) fear   (d) memory   (e) passion

6 (a) golf   (b) tennis   (c) boxing   (d) football   (e) rugby

7 (a) learning (b) scholarship (c) university (d) erudition
   (e) studiousness

8 (a) penguin (b) bat (c) robin (d) mayfly (e) eagle

9 (a) blue (b) cyan (c) yellow (d) green (e) indigo

10 (a) tilde (b) ampersand (c) asterisk (d) hyperlink
   (e) circumflex

Become a word dynamo! Find out your word power, and increase it with the tests and games at http://dynamo.dictionary.com/.

Verbal test 3: Vocabulary

Meanings

1 A **foible** is a:
   (a) strength   (b) mistake   (c) slight fault
   (d) misunderstanding

2 Turpitude is:
   (a) laziness   (b) depravity   (c) brush cleaner (d) beauty

3 A **sextant** is most likely to be used by a:
   (a) doctor   (b) prostitute   (c) navigator   (d) astronomer

4 An **esoteric** word is:
   (a) rude   (b) unusual   (c) erotic   (d) foreign

5 To impede is to:
   (a) hinder   (b) help   (c) enrage   (d) anger

Antonyms

Choose the word with the opposite meaning:

6 Dextrous
(a) sinister   (b) clumsy   (c) valuable   (d) fragile

7 Aerate
(a) suffocate   (b) placate   (c) transmit   (d) argue

8 Harmony
(a) accord   (b) solo   (c) discord   (d) error

9 Paucity
(a) beauty   (b) doubt   (c) modesty   (d) excess

10 Dilettante
(a) plotter   (b) aesthete   (c) professional   (d) austere

Verbal test 4: Mixed bag

1 Which pair of words has the same relationship as **cottage** has to **residence**?

   (a) flat: apartment   (b) oak: tree   (c) castle: tower   (d) tent: field

2 Which pair of words has the same relationship as **plough** has to **cow**?

   (a) fox: hound   (b) track: runner   (c) course: horse   (d) field: sheep

3 Which pair of words has the same relationship as **enraged** has to **grenade**?

   (a) peaceful: bullet   (b) random: clued
   (c) anger: explode   (d) master: stream

4 Which pair of words has the same relationship as **colour** has to **spectrum**?

   (a) waves: sound   (b) verse: rhyme   (c) tone: scale   (d) noise: waves

5 Which pair of words has the same relationship as **cut** has to **knife**?

   (a) drill: bit   (b) shovel: dig   (c) fork: impale   (d) hole: spade

34

Which is the odd word out?

6 (a) rain (b) sleet (c) storm (d) snow (e) hail

7 (a) rotor (b) civic (c) racecar (d) ford (e) radar

8 (a) flow (b) snip (c) trap (d) draw (e) back

9 (a) answer (b) simple (c) lamb (d) straight

10 (a) wool (b) cotton (c) leather (d) silk

Online testing
www.queendom.com/ has a well-structured
and validated online verbal intelligence test.
What's your score?

4 Numbers count

Numeric ability

Numeric intelligence tests do measure how well you did at maths at school – but only to a very small extent. They mainly measure the brain's processing speed and working memory. The only number skills you normally need are counting, simple addition, subtraction and multiplication. What matters more is your ability to recognize patterns and relationships within and between numbers, and to juggle a bunch of numbers in your head quickly.

Numeric tests can be based on:

* **Sequences**, where you have to find the next value or a missing one. These can sometimes be alphabetic, e.g. **a, c, e, g, i** … where the problem is to find the number of letters between the steps.

* **Calculations**, either in the form of 'real life' problems or finding missing values from grids.
* Numbers as **digits** rather than **values**, e.g. so that 25 can be treated as $(2 \times 10) + 5$, or as the digits 2 and 5, which could be added to make 7, or subtracted to give −3 or multiplied to give 10, etc.

If you've forgotten the maths you (half-)learned at school, and now find that you need it again, you might like to try this Teach Yourself book: *Great at my Job but Crap at Numbers*, by Mac Bride and Heidi Smith. Find out more at www.crapatnumbers.net.

Numeric intelligence tests ... mainly measure the brain's speed and working memory

Numeric test 1: Sequences

At the simplest, a sequence has the same value missing between each pair:

> 1, 4, 7, 10, 13, 16 …

The numbers go up in steps of 3.

The step values can change according to a pattern:

> 1, 2, 4, 7, 11, 16 …

The steps here are 1, 2, 3, 4, 5.

There may be a pattern of calculations:

> 25, 52, 77, 77, 154, 451, …

Reverse the digits to create a new number, add that to the previous one, and repeat.

There may be two or more interwoven sequences:

> **50**, 1, **45**, 5, **40**, 9, **35** …, …

The odd numbers are going down 5 at a time; the even numbers are going up 4 at a time.

What's next?

1 1, 1, 2, 3, 5, 8, 13, 21, ?
   (a) 30   (b) 34   (c) 36   (d) 42

2 12, 24, 36, 72, 108, 216, ?
   (a) 288   (b) 144   (c) 432   (d) 324

3 11, 12, 14, 19, 20, 23, 28, 29, 33, ?
   (a) 34   (b) 39   (c) 38   (d) 40

4 1, 2, 4, 6, 9, 12, 15, 19, 23, 27, 31, ?
   (a) 35   (b) 40   (c) 37   (d) 36

5 25, 20, 21, 17, 19, 16 , 19, ?
   (a) 17   (b) 21   (c) 15   (d) 18

Numeric test 2: Calculations

Sometimes when faced with a numeric problem – in a test or in real life – you do not need to work it out properly. It may be enough to check that it's the right size, or ends in the right digit, e.g. are these correct?

(a) $135 + 47 = 186$

(b) $23 \times 159 = 2007$

(c) $714 - 308 = 406$

(a) must be wrong, because $5 + 7 = 12$, so the last digit should be 2.

(b) must be wrong, because $20 \times 100 = 2000$, so 23×159 must be a lot bigger than that.

(c) is right.

In the following problems, use shortcuts where possible.

Pick the correct answer

1 $16 + 46 = 6 + ?$
    (a) 55 (b) 56 (c) 66 (d) 67

2 $44 - ? = 15$
    (a) 29 (b) 26 (c) 28 (d) 39

3 $210 \div 35 = ?$
    (a) 5 (b) 5.5 (c) 6 (d) 6.4

4 The bill in a restaurant is £12.50 (starters) £25.88 (mains) £15.40 (drinks). With a 10% tip, what is the total cost?
    (a) £59.16   (b) £61.28
    (c) £55.14   (d) £57.75

5 If eight machines make 15,000 widgets a week, how many can four machines make in 4 weeks?
    (a) 60,000   (b) 25,000
    (c) 32,000   (d) 30,000

True (a) or false (b)?

6 $13 \times 24 = 312$

7 $76 \div 3 = 22$

8 $828 + 452 = 1180$

9 $37 + 3 - 15 - 7 + 21 - 14 = 25$

10 $(3 \times 7) - 12 - (6 \times 2) + 3 = 0$

Numeric test 3: Values and digits

In IQ tests, a number is not necessarily to be taken as a value.

✳ Q: What do **279** and **628** have in common? A: You can add the first two digits to get the third.

✳ Q: In the pattern **19: 61, 68: XX**, what is the missing number? A: 89. The digits have been turned 180°.

✳ Q: Which is the odd one out: 1368, 1863, 3671, 8613? A: 3671. The others use the same digits.

Remember this as you do the next test.

1 What is the missing number?

294	722	428
583	790	207
737	?	135

(a) 843 (b) 736 (c) 872 (d) 602

2 What is the missing number?

24	35	48
63	42	54
82	51	?

(a) 66 (b) 62 (c) 72 (d) 60

3 What is the missing number?

5783	5873	3857
3546	3456	6435
5493	?	3954

(a) 5943   (b) 9543   (c) 3459   (d) 5934

4 What is the missing number?

63	20	29
15	10	22
42	26	47

35	16	62
18	?	20
82	22	57

(a) 19   (b) 11   (c) 38   (d) 18

5 What comes next: 347, 528, 634, 752, 863, ?
(a) 983   (b) 957   (c) 475   (d) 575

Numeric test 4: Mixed bag

1 What comes next: 1, 1, 7, 4, 13, 7, 19, 10, …
(a) 23 (b) 25 (c) 16 (d) 29

2 What comes next: 100, 86.6, 73.2, 59.8, 46.4, …
(a) 34.6 (b) 35.2
(c) 32.8 (d) 33

3 What is the missing number?

5	8	6	7
3	2	6	8
4	4	5	6
2	3	3	?

(a) 2 (b) 9 (c) 7 (d) 4

4 Which block will fill the space?

7	4	11	15
11			35
9		16	23

(a)

19	27
7	

(b)

8	13
6	

(c)

12	23
7	

(d)

9	18
13	

5 What is the missing number: 4672, 3496, 595

    (a) 2   (b) 4   (c) 3   (d) 7

6 What is the missing number?

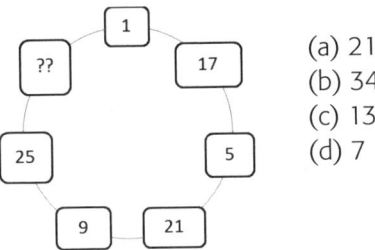

    (a) 21
    (b) 34
    (c) 13
    (d) 7

7 What is the missing number?

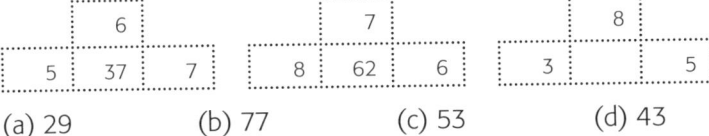

    (a) 29   (b) 77   (c) 53   (d) 43

8 What comes next? 1, 2, 5, 14, 41, …

    (a) 114   (b) 95   (c) 55   (d) 122

5 Sight and insight

Visual/spatial intelligence

Problems are designed to extend your ability to:

* see relationships and patterns
* visualize how two-dimensional objects will appear when transformed in various ways
* visualize and manipulate three-dimensional objects

The so-called 'culture-free' IQ tests often concentrate on visual–spatial problems as these are less affected by schooling and home background. But familiarity and practice do make a difference. Making paper models and playing with Lego helps to build a child's 2D to 3D visualization.

Familiarity and practice make a difference

Practice helps

Which of these shapes could be the plan?

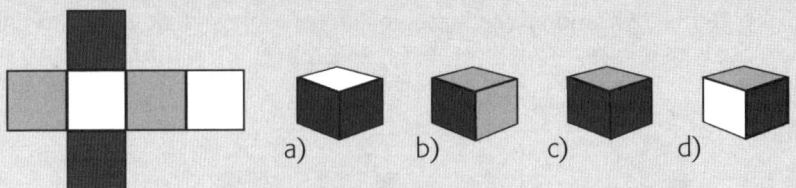

a) b) c) d)

If you struggle when faced with something like this, try making some paper models. You can find plans for cubes, pyramids, cylinders and the like on the Web (search for 'paper models 3D solids'). Colour the sides before you fold them and try to work out how they will look.

An intelligence test sometimes shows a man how smart he would have been not to have taken it.

Laurence Peter

Visual test 1: Seeing patterns

The questions in this section test your ability to deduce relationships, patterns and sequences. Some are similar to those that you met earlier, but with images instead of words or numbers.

1 What comes next?

   　　a) 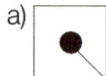　b) 　c)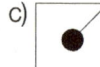

2 What comes next?

   　　a) 　b) 　c)

3 Which is the missing image for the second pair?

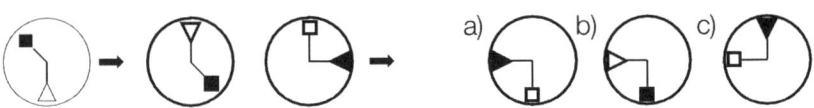

4 Which is the missing image for the second pair?

5 Which is the odd one out?

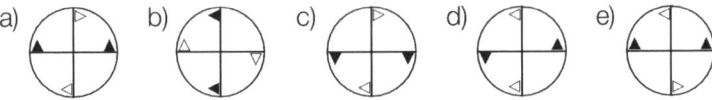

Visual test 2: Visualization

In these problems, images are being transformed in some way, and to solve them you need to be able to visualize the transformations in your head – turn them over, look at them the other way up, recolour them, or whatever.

1 What comes next?

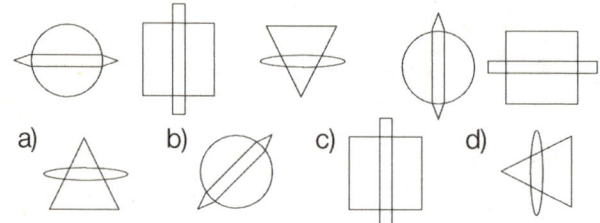

a)   b)   c)   d)

2 Which three pieces can be assembled to make a triangle?

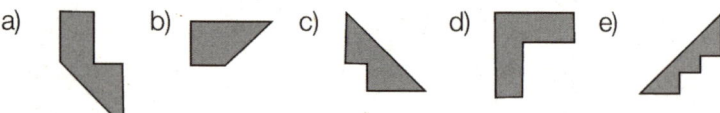

a)   b)   c)   d)   e)

54

3 Two images can be combined to make a new one, following certain rules. What image should result from the second pair?

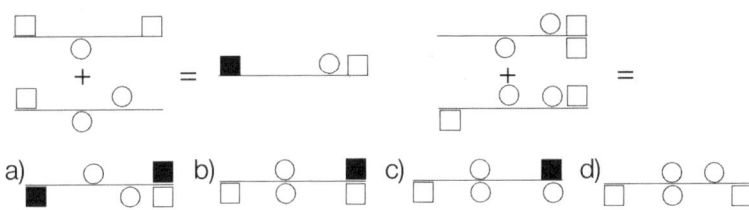

a)   b)   c)   d)

4 How many rectangles can you find in this diagram?

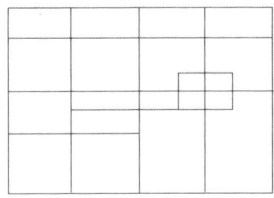

5 What is the missing image?

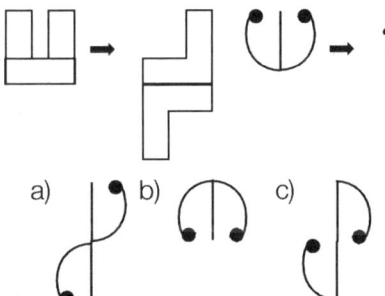

a)   b)   c)

Visual test 3: 3D visualization

1 Which of the plans can be folded to make the cube?

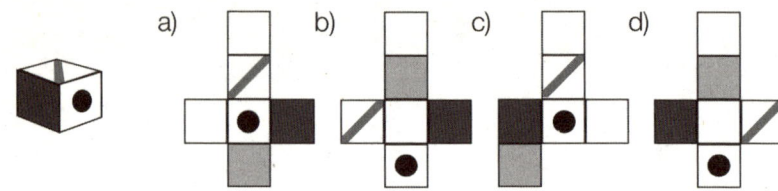

a)   b)   c)   d)

2 How many cubes are in this stack?

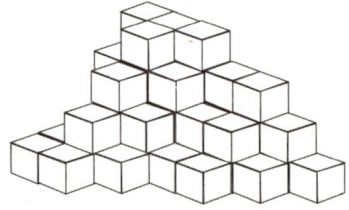

3 Which model matches the plans?

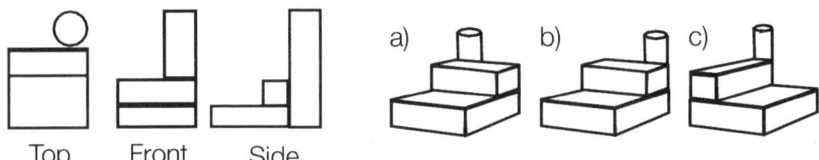

Top   Front   Side

a)   b)   c)

4 What comes next?

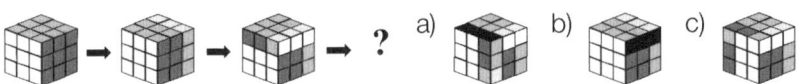

?   a)   b)   c)

5 If you fold along the dotted line, what comes next?

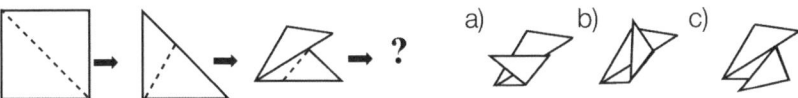

?   a)   b)   c)

Visual test 4: Mixed bag

1 How many lines?

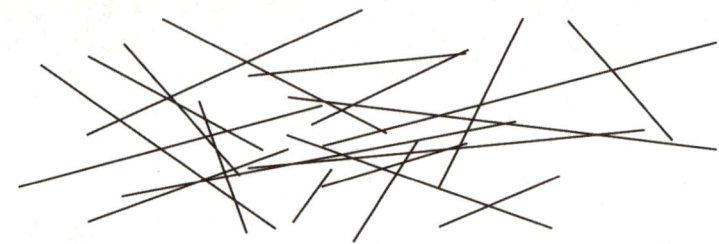

2 What comes next?

3 Which is the odd one out?

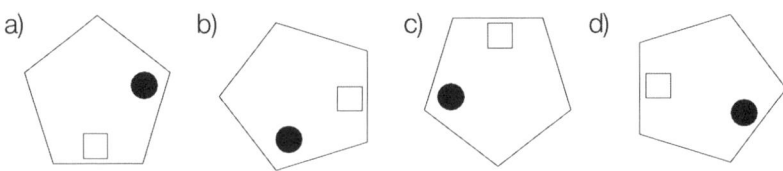

a) b) c) d)

4 Which is the third piece of this 3D jigsaw?

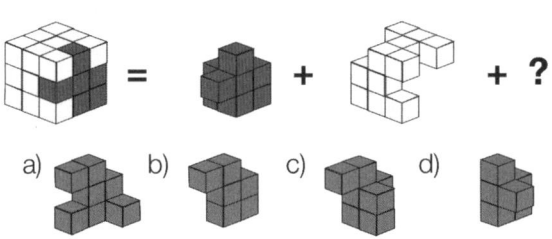

a) b) c) d)

6 Logical thinking

Logical problems

When tackling logical problems read them carefully and think about each part. The setter may be out to mislead!

✳ If one thing follows another, is it cause and effect?

Jo went to the beach. It rained. Is Jo a rain god?

✳ Coincidence proves nothing.

I surround my house with breadcrumbs and the tigers stay away. Do breadcrumbs deter tigers?

✳ Just because two related statements are true, it doesn't follow that a third related statement must also be true.

Fido likes bones. Dogs like bones. Therefore Fido is a dog. True? Not necessarily. Fido could be a tiger.

✳ Beware of multiple meanings.

What goes up must come down. Harry is up before the judge. Therefore Harry will go down. True?

✳ Setting out the problem on paper, in simple words or as a diagram, may help to clarify your thinking.

Sally is three times as old as Peter. In 4 years she will be twice as old as him. How old are they? This can be expressed mathematically as:

(i) $S = 3P$ and (ii) $S + 4 = 2(P + 4)$

And a bit of simple algebra: $P = 4$ and $S = 12$.

The setter may be out to mislead!

Logic test 1: True, false or not proven?

In these problems you will be given three or more statements, and the question is whether the last one is true or false or not proven – because sometimes there simply isn't enough information.

1 Clara is older than Cathy. Conor was born before Clara. Therefore Cathy is younger than Conor. True, false or not proven?

2 Where there's poverty, there's theft. There's theft in Wall Street. Therefore there's poverty in Wall Street. True, false or not proven?

3 Vegans do not eat cheese. Sam is eating cheese. Therefore Sam is not vegan. True, false or not proven?

4 Vegans eat beans. Sam is eating beans. Therefore Sam is vegan. True, false or not proven?

Does this follow?

The question here is whether the first statements lead to a conclusion.

5 If Jack takes the cow to market, he may get some magic beans. If Jack has some magic beans, he may get the golden goose. Jack has taken the cow to market. Will Jack get the golden goose?

6 Dick was stabbed to death in his flat. Jo was seen entering and leaving his flat around the time of his death. No-one else was seen entering or leaving. Jo's fingerprints and Dick's blood were found on a knife near the body. Did Jo kill Dick?

Logic: The art of thinking and reasoning in strict accordance with the limitations and incapacities of the human misunderstanding.

Ambrose Bierce

Logic test 2: Place and logic

Visualization and spatial reasoning ability also come into these problems (drawing them on paper is allowed!)

1 Get your ducks in a row! In what order are the five ducks?

* Daffy is two places behind Donald
* Dicky is three places behind Daisy
* Dido is after Daffy.

2 These four cards should follow the rule: 'if a card has an even number on one side, it must have a circle on the other'. Which must you turn over to check that the rule has been obeyed?

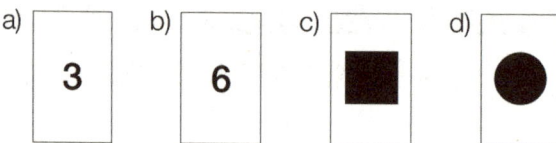

a) 3 b) 6 c) ■ d) ●

3   There are five people of different heights. Alan is taller than David, who is taller than Ellie. Carol is shorter than Bob, but taller than Alan. Who is the third tallest person?

4   There is a water lily in the centre of a pond. It doubles in size every day, and fills the pond after 20 days. If it was 30 cm wide on day 1, how much of the pond does it cover on day 19?

> Question 2 is a variation of the Wason selection task, devised by Peter Cathcart Wason, one of the great thinkers in the field of the psychology of reasoning.

Logic will get you from A to B. Imagination will take you everywhere.

Albert Einstein

Logic test 3: Pants on fire

Who can you trust nowadays? Only yourself and your own powers of logical deduction. Use them to work out who's telling the truth in these problems.

1 'They are all liars around here, except me,' said Mrs Jones. Her neighbour added, 'That's true.'

Are they all liars around there, except for Mrs Jones?

2 MI6 is leaking like a sieve. They have narrowed the suspects down to three, who make the following statements.

✳ George: 'Tony is a mole.'
✳ Tony: 'Peter is a mole.'
✳ Peter: 'Tony is lying.'

Assuming that moles lie and non-moles tell the truth:

a If there is only one mole, who is it?
b If there are two moles, who are they?

3 Only one of these four statements is true. Which one?

   a There is one false statement in this set.
   b There are two false statements in this set.
   c There are three false statements in this set.
   d There are four false statements in this set.

4 A traveller reaches a fork in the road. One way leads to the Desert of Despair, the other to the Oasis of Ouzo. Two locals are at the fork. The traveller knows that one is a liar and one tells the truth, but he doesn't know which is which. He wants to get to the oasis. What question does he ask which local?

A lie can run around the world six times while the truth is still trying to put on its pants.
Mark Twain

Logic test 4: Mixed bag

1   Pursued by orcs through the dark night, the hobbits reach a chasm. There is a narrow rickety bridge over it, but it will take only the weight of two hobbits at a time. They will need a torch to get over safely, but have only one torch, and the chasm is too wide to throw the torch across. The hobbits move at different speeds. Bilbo can cross in 1 minute, Chico in 2 minutes, Dido in 4 minutes and Frito in 8 minutes. The orcs will catch up with them in 15 minutes. How can they all get safely across?

2   The fuse has gone, so it's pitch black upstairs. A student is getting ready to go out. There are three pairs of shoes under the bed, and 27 socks, a mixture of red and white, in his drawer. How many socks and shoes must he take downstairs into the light to be sure of having matching pairs of socks and of shoes?

3   Can a man legally marry his widow's sister?

4 This oval building has two doors to the outside and four to the inner courtyard. Can you get from A to B by going through each door once only?

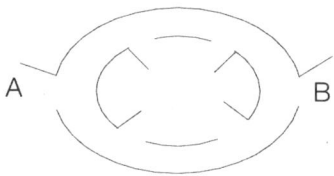

5 This one has only three doors to the inner courtyard. Can you get from A to B, passing through each door only once?

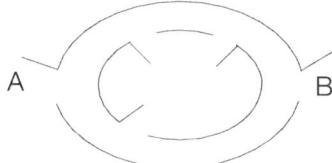

7 Creative thinking

Using the left brain

Logical, spatial and verbal reasoning will get you a long way in solving problems, but they are not always enough. Sometimes you need to think creatively, or divergently.

Convergent and divergent thinking

In *convergent* thinking, you focus on the problem, analyse its components, and follow logical steps through to the solution.

In *divergent* thinking, you look at the problem from the top, sides and bottom, and bring in ideas from outside to find the solution – or solutions – for a divergent approach. You may find more than one (see diagram opposite).

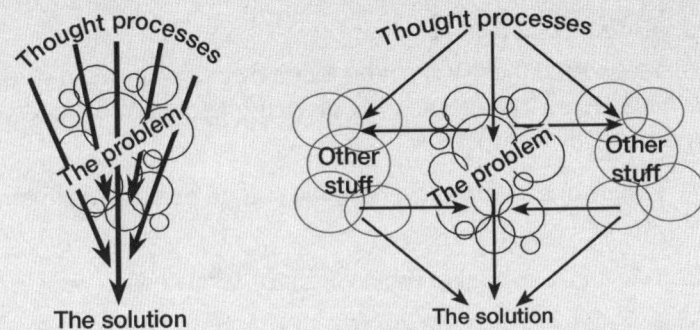

Thought processes

The problem

The solution

Thought processes

Other stuff

Other stuff

The problem

The solution

Reasoning is not always enough to solve problems

Thinking is the hardest work there is, which is probably the reason so few engage in it.

Henry Ford

Creative test 1

The answers to these will not be found by following a train of logic. Think carefully about the real meaning of each question. Where a situation is described, try to visualize it.

1 You are in a race and overtake the second person. What position are you in?

2 If you overtake the last person in a race, what position would you be in?

3 Which word is the odd one out and why? There are at least two possible answers to this.

   scowl   deprecate   trample   celebrate   demean

4 What comes next in this sequence?

5 Why do Chinese men eat more rice than Japanese men?

6 The foreman told the carpenter, 'Four of the locks on these first eight doors are faulty.' The carpenter went to the one lock he knew was faulty and fixed that, then started to hunt for the other three. Where did he start?

7 A rectangular cake has had a rectangular piece removed from it. How would you cut the remainder into two equal halves with one straight cut of a knife?

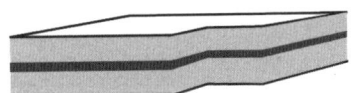

Creative thinking is not a talent, it is a skill that can be learnt.
Edward de Bono

Creative test 2

Sometimes, when searching for a creative solution, it is better not to focus on the problem. Make sure that you understand it thoroughly, then put it to one side and do something else. Go for a walk, bake a cake, have a bath and let your subconscious mind mull it over.

1   How can you plant 10 trees in five straight lines, with four in each line?

2   A ladder hangs over the side of a yacht, with its bottom rung 10 cm below the water. The ladder is 2 metres long, and the rungs are 20 cm apart. The tide is rising at the rate of 30 cm an hour. When will the water reach the third rung from the top?

3   Two boys were born on the same date and same year to the same mother, but are not twins. Can you explain that?

4 Your ping pong ball bounced down the narrow cylindrical hole where the clothes post usually stands. The hole is 5 mm wider than the ball. You have the bats, the net and your backpack, containing spare socks, a ballpoint pen, a notebook and a water bottle. How can you get the ball out of the hole?

5 A hermit has only one clock in his house and no TV, Internet access, telephone or any other way to tell the time. One day he wakes up to find that the clock has stopped – he forgot to wind it up. He starts it again, setting it to 12.00, then walks 2 miles along the road to his friend's house. When he came back later, he was able to set his clock correctly. How?

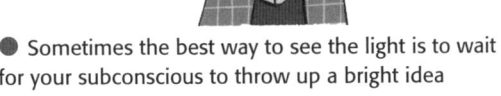

● Sometimes the best way to see the light is to wait for your subconscious to throw up a bright idea

Creative test 3

If you're stuck on a problem, try this to kick start your thinking. Pick up any object at random, or take a word from the dictionary, and make a connection between it and the problem. It doesn't matter how forced that connection is, the simple fact of looking at the problem from a different perspective will sometimes trigger the new thoughts you need to find a solution.

1 To the nearest cubic centimetre, how much soil is there in a 3m × 2.5m × 2m hole?

2 How can you throw a ball as hard as you can, and make it stop and return to you, without hitting anything and with nothing attached to it?

3 There are two clocks. One gains an hour every hour, the other loses an hour every hour. Which tells the right time the most often?

4 What can you put in a box that would make it lighter? Why would putting more in make it lighter still?

5 Heard in a hardware store:

* 'How much for one?'
* 'Two pounds, madam'
* 'And how much for 10?'
* 'Four pounds'
* 'How much for 100?'
* 'Six pounds, madam'
* What was the woman buying?

6 Name four days beginning with 'T'.

7 By moving one glass only, arrange these glasses so that the full ones are all next to each other.

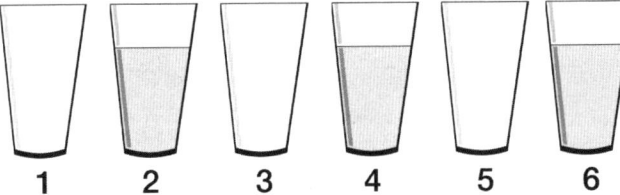

1   2   3   4   5   6

Creative test 4

A second head often helps. If you explain a problem and your attempts to solve it to someone else, the solution may well come to you while you are talking. The other person does not need to say anything – simply listen. In fact, talking to the cat can work just as well.

1 Why are round manhole covers better than square ones?

2 It's a wet and windy night. Driving along the road you pass a bus stop where three people are waiting:

* One is a frail old lady who looks very ill.
* One is a man who once saved your life.
* The third is the soulmate you met once but were cruelly parted from and have not been able to find since.

   Your car will only take one passenger. To whom do you give a lift?

3 Driving your car home the next day, you get a puncture. While changing the wheel, you step back on the hubcap, where you've put the nuts, and flip all four of them down the nearest drain. They are lost. Is there any way to drive the car home?

4 A closed, windowless room has three lights inside, controlled by three switches outside. If you are only allowed to go into the room once, how can you tell which switch operates which light?

5 Join the dots with four straight lines, each new one starting where the previous stopped.

8 Brain stretchers

Quickies, trickies and classics

Here are some puzzles to get your brain working: some quickies, some tricky ones and some classics. Treat this first set as a warm-up – you might want to commit some of these to memory to try out on friends later.

Warm-ups

1 When the policeman saw the bus driver going the wrong way down a one-way street, why didn't he stop him.

2 A lorry has reached a bridge where the clearance is 5 cm less than the height of the lorry. The alternative route will take an extra 4 hours. Is there any way to avoid this?

3 There are six apples in a box. Six boys take one each. Why is there still one left in the box?

4 Divide 50 by half and add 20. What's the total?

5 Why can't a woman living in Wales by buried in England?

6 Mary's mother has four children. The first three are called April, May and June. What's the fourth called?

7 An adult penguin weighs 7 kg. A polar bear can eat 10 kg of meat in 15 minutes. How many penguins can a polar bear eat in 1 hour?

8 It's dark. You have an oil lamp, a candle and firewood but only one match. Which do you light first?

9 I had 12 bottles of beer: Jake drank three, John drank four, Will drank all but two. How many have I left?

10 What can most people hold in their right hand, but not in their left.

11 If ↓→→ equals 'see', what does ↑→←↓ equal?

12 You have two iron bars, one of which is magnetized. How can you tell which one?

Common sense is not so common.
Voltaire

Einstein's grid puzzle

When Albert Einstein created this puzzle, he estimated that only 2% of people would be able to solve it. That means that there is a solution, so go for it!

In a street there are five houses, painted five different colours.

In each house lives a person of different nationality, and each has a different preferred drink and brand of cigarette and keeps a different pet.

Working from the following information, who keeps fish?

* The Brit lives in a red house.
* The Swede keeps dogs as pets.
* The Dane drinks tea.
* The green house is next to, and on the left of, the white house.
* The owner of the green house drinks coffee.
* The person who smokes Pall Mall rears birds.
* The owner of the yellow house smokes Dunhill.

* The man living in the centre house drinks milk.
* The Norwegian lives in the first house.
* The man who smokes blends lives next to the one who keeps cats.
* The man who keeps horses lives next to the man who smokes Dunhill.
* The man who smokes Blue Master drinks beer.
* The German smokes Prince.
* The Norwegian lives next to the blue house.
* The man who smokes blends has a neighbour who drinks water.

TOP TIP

To solve these grid puzzles, draw a 5 × 5 grid on a sheet of paper and write into the cells the things you are sure about (in ink) and what may be (in pencil). Go through the list several times, first to identify what must be, then what might be. Pure logic will get you to the solution.

Grid puzzle 2

How about another of those? You may find this a touch easier.

There are five bespoke birthday cakes on the shelf at the baker's, ready for delivery.

Which one is coffee flavoured? Which one is going to Ealing?

* Sandy is 21 and her cake is chocolate flavoured.
* The cake in the middle has pink icing.
* Dandy's cake is for her 40th birthday.
* Candy's cake has white icing and is to the left of the chocolate one.
* To the right of the vanilla-flavoured cake is one going to Pinewood.
* Andy's cake is to be delivered to Elstree.
* Next to the strawberry-flavoured cake is one with yellow icing.

* The cake going to Shepperton has two candles.
* Mandy's 90th birthday cake is to the right of the one going to Pinewood.
* The cake with brown icing is to be delivered to Camberwell.
* Next to the cake with 90 candles is one with green icing.
* The cake at the far right is banana flavoured.
* The cake with pink icing has 10 candles.
* The banana-flavoured cake is next to the strawberry-flavoured one.
* The cake going to Camberwell has 21 candles.

It's not that I'm so smart, it's just that I stay with problems longer.

Albert Einstein

Euler puzzles

Leonhard Euler was an 18th-century mathematician whose theories are behind much of modern maths. One of the areas he explored was topology, which is about lines, nodes (junctions) and planes. A whole set of puzzles sprang from this work. Here are four. In each case the challenge is to find a way of drawing the diagram without taking your pencil off the paper, and without going over any line twice. It is not always possible.

> Three of these are possible.

1

2

3

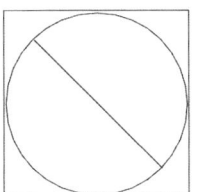

4

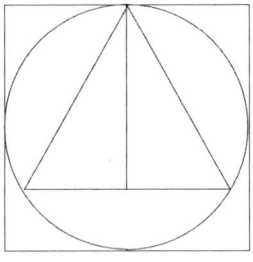

Sam Loyd puzzles

Sam Lloyd was a 19th-century American setter of mathematical and chess problems. His puzzles are still capable of stretching brains. Try these for starters.

1 On the way out to the great annual picnic, every wagon in town was in use. Half-way there, 10 wagons broke down, and each of the remaining wagons took one more person. When they started for home, 15 more wagons were broken, and the rest had to take another two passengers.

   How many people went to the picnic?

2 While riding on the carousel, Sammy, who was good at sums, noticed this: 'One-third of the number of kids riding ahead of me, added to three-quarters of those riding behind me, gives the correct number of children on this merry-go-round.'

   How many riders were there?

3 At the archery contest, the challenge was to score 100 points, using as many arrows as necessary. Is it possible?

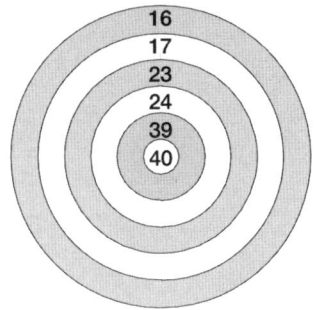

4 Four men sat down and played together all evening for money. At the end of the evening all four were £50 better off. How can that be?

5 A man goes to a bank with a cheque for $200 and says to the cashier 'Give me some one-dollar bills, ten times as many twos and the balance in fives'. What does the cashier give him?

If you enjoyed tackling these, Sam Loyd's *Cyclopedia of Puzzles* is still in print, and you can find it on the Web at www.mathpuzzle.com/loyd/

9 Making better memories

From goldfish to elephant

They say that goldfish have a 20-second memory and that elephants never forget. Neither of these is true, but why let that spoil a good heading!

If you don't do anything to stop the process, roughly half of what you learn will be forgotten within 20 minutes, and two-thirds within 2 days. The good news is, you can turn yourself from a goldfish into an elephant – in memory terms, at least.

You can turn yourself from a goldfish into an elephant

From short- to long-term memory

In this section we will look at ways to ensure that information is captured from short-term memory, where it will be forgotten in seconds, and stored in long-term memory, where it will stay safe forever. The key techniques are:

* Focus and fix the experience.
* Process the information.
* Add impact by involving more sense.
* Refresh memories before they fade.

Nothing fixes a thing so intensely in the memory as the wish to forget it.

Michel de Montaigne

Focus and fix

The next time you want to remember something, pay attention. The aim is to forge strong initial synapses – you want to get those dendrites well hooked on to the axons.

✱ If it's an image/face/object/scene – really look at it. Trace the outlines with your eyes, look at the details, see how the parts form a whole.

✱ If it's a speaker/music/birdsong – focus on that sound and ignore anything else around. Listen to every word or note.

✱ If it's a phone number, email address, directions or similar item of information, say it to yourself if you are reading it, or visualize it written down if you are hearing it.

● Look closely if you want to remember

The true art of memory is the art of attention.

Samuel Johnson

Attention span

We all have a limited attention span, so don't try to fight it:

* For a 2-year old child, the limit is about 5 minutes
* For a healthy adult, the limit is around 20 minutes.

If the motivation is there, attention can be refocused continually – you'd never see the end of a movie otherwise. If a high level of attention and effort is needed, e.g. when learning something new, take a break every 20 minutes or so to recharge the batteries.

To remember something, pay attention

Process the information

For information to be transferred from short- to long-term memory it must be **encoded** or categorized in some way. The more we can make sense of something, the easier it is to remember.

One of the ways in which we encode new information is through **schema**. These are standard patterns that you can fit the new data into, so that you need only remember the specifics as you already have the shape. You don't need to remember that someone has two eyes, a nose and a mouth – that's part of the face schema – just the colour of the eyes and shape of the nose and mouth.

The more we can make sense of something, the easier it is to remember

Add a sense, add impact

Sight

Simonides, the father of the art of memory, realized that sight makes the strongest memories. If you can add an image to an idea, it's easier to remember than words alone. The ancient Greeks generally used images of people – but enhanced in some way. They might be caricatured, or wearing vivid colours, or making exaggerated gestures, or whatever.

Sound

To strengthen the memory of something you have seen, add sound. You will remember a place name better if you say it aloud. To help fix a scene, describe it to yourself, summarising it with key words or phrases.

Scents and other senses

These are much harder to add purely in your imagination – can you conjure up the smell of vanilla or the touch of velvet? But if you can capture any other sensations alongside the thing you are trying to memorize, they will help to fix it – and may help to stimulate recall later.

Making connections

Unconnected individual items are the hardest things to remember. If you can connect the thing you want to remember to something that you already know, it will be much easier to remember it and to recall it later. This simple fact lies at the bottom of most memory techniques.

The basic technique here is to link one item to the next by creating a narrative with vivid mental images. For example, suppose that you need to shop for:

* a cauliflower
* a box of matches
* bathroom cleaner
* a colour cartridge for the printer.

Imagine a small pan overflowing with cauliflower florets. The gas needs lighting, so you strike a huge match. To put it out, you plunge it in the bath – which now needs cleaning. You splash the cleaner on to a towel and it bleaches it white. You'll have to put it into the printer to put the pattern back.

Run the 'movie' through a couple of times and it should be fixed. As long as you can remember the pan full of cauliflower, you will remember all the other items.

104

Be vivid

Your narratives do not have to make sense, and the imaginary world does not have to follow the normal rules – you don't need to think, for example, about how you get from the cooker to the bath. Just turn around and it will be there. What counts is that it is memorable. The more vivid you can make the images the better. Make them any or all of:

* brightly coloured
* overlarge
* obscene
* ridiculous
* loud.

A linked list is easy to create, but has two drawbacks:

* If you forget the start point, you've had it.
* You need to work through the list to find each item.

I have a memory like an elephant. In fact, elephants often consult me.
Noel Coward

Refresh and remember

If you are trying to learn stuff, you need to fix the knowledge before it fades. There are optimal points at which to do this – it's basically a matter of catching the synaptic connections before they decay and reinforcing them:

* **10 minutes** after you start, take a minute or two to review what you have just read, heard or viewed. This is almost a part of the initial processing that encodes the information.
* **1 day** after, skim through the material again, paying special attention to anything that you are unsure about.
* **1 week** after, review again – and be pleased at how much you have retained.
* **1 month**, and then **6 months** after, refresh the information.

You should find that after the 6-month refresher, the information should be more or less permanently etched into your synapses.

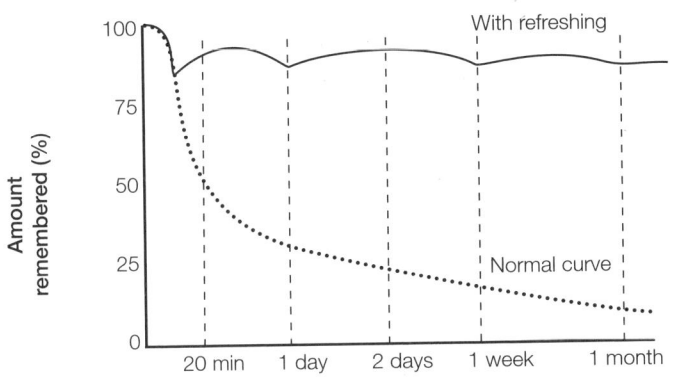

New information is quickly forgotten if you don't take steps to reinforce the memory.

If you are trying to learn stuff, you need to fix the knowledge

10 Answers

Chapter 3

Verbal test 1 1 (c), 2 (d), 3 (b), 4 (c), 5 (d), 6 (a), 7 (b), 8 (c), 9 (d), 10 (a).

Verbal test 2 1 (b), 2 (d), 3 (a), 4 (e), 5 (d), 6 (c), 7 (c), 8 (a), 9 (b), 10 (d).

Verbal test 3 1 (c), 2 (b), 3 (c), 4 (b), 5 (a), 6 (b), 7 (a), 8 (c), 9 (d), 10 (c).

Verbal test 4 1 (b), 2 (c), 3 (d), 4 (c), 5 (a), 6 (c) – not a type of precipitation, 7 (d) – not a palindrome, 8 (e) – does not make another word when read backwards, 9 (b) – no silent letter, 10 (b) – vegetable origin.

Chapter 4

Numeric test 1 1 (b) – add two numbers to make the next; 2 (d) – two series, each × 3; 3 (c) – steps are 1,2,5, 1,3,5, 1,4,5, etc.; 4 (d) – steps are 1, 2, 2, 3, 3, 3, 4, 4, 4, 4, 5, etc.; 5 (a) – steps are −5, +1, −4, +2, −3, +3, −2, +4.

Numeric test 2 1 (b), 2 (a), 3 (c), 4 (a), 5 (d), 6 (a), 7 (b), 8 (b), 9 (a), 10 (a).

Numeric test 3 1 (c) – add the left and right values; 2 (d) – add the digits of the numbers in the first two columns and multiply $(8 + 2) \times (5 + 1) = 60$; 3 (a) – order of digits is changed to a set pattern; 4 (b) – add the digits of the numbers in the side column, and top and bottom rows, to get the central figures; 5 (c) – the digits 3475286 are repeated in the same order.

Numeric test 4 1 (b) – two intermixed series, adding 6 and 3; 2 (d) – subtract 13.4 each time; 3 (a) – the columns total 14, 17, 20 – next must be 23; 4 (c) – add columns 1 and 2 to get column 3, and add columns 2 and 3 to get column 4; 5 (b) – multiply the middle numbers to get the one shown in the outside digits; 6 (c) – starting from 1, jump a number and add 4 to the next; 7 (a) – multiply top and left numbers, then add the one on the right; 8 (d) – multiply by 3 and subtract 1 to get the next.

Chapter 5

Visual test 1 1 (c), 2 (b), 3 (a), 4 (c), 5 (e).

Visual test 2 1 (d) – the first three images, are repeated with a 90°
turn; 2 (a), (c) and (d); 3 (c) – when the images are overlaid, if two
squares are in the same place, they go black; if two circles overlap they
disappear; 4 – 39; 5 (a) – the left half is folded down.

Visual test 3 1 (c), 2 50, 3 (b), 4 (a), 5 (b).

Visual test 4 1 – 21, 2 (b), 3 (d), 4 (b).

Chapter 6

Logic test 1 1 true; 2 not proven; 3 true; 4 not proven; 5 not
necessarily – if it had said 'he *will* get …' and not 'he *may* get …' then
the answer would have been 'Yes'; 6 not necessarily – Dick could have
been killed by someone who was still in the flat or who left without
being seen, or it may have been suicide.

Logic test 2 1 Donald, Daisy, Daffy, Dido, Dicky. 2 (b) and (c). You don't need to check (a) as it is has an odd number – what's on the other side is irrelevant. You don't need to check (d) because the rule does not prevent odd numbers being backed by a circle. You do need to check that (b) has a circle and that (c) does not have an even number. 3 Alan – in order of height they are Bob, Carol, Alan, David, Ellie. 4 Half the pond. It then doubles to fill the whole pond. The initial size is irrelevant and it is there just to distract you.

Logic test 3 1 If Mrs Jones was telling the truth, then her neighbour must be lying. But if her neighbour was lying, then what Mrs Jones said was not true. Mrs Jones must also be a liar. 2 (a) George and Peter are both saying that Tony is a mole/liar. If there is only one mole, it must be Tony. If there are two, they must be George and Peter. 3 (c) Only one is true, therefore three must be false. 4 A straight 'Which way to the oasis?' carries a 50% chance of being pointed into the desert. The trick is to frame the question so that you know that there's a lie in the answer, then discount it. So, the traveller should ask either local, 'If I asked her which way, what would she tell me?', and go the other way. The truth teller will pass on the liar's lie; the liar will invert the truth teller's good direction.

Logic test 4 1 Getting the torch back is the problem. If the two fastest cross first, then that gets the torch back fastest. The pattern, and elapsed time, is: B and C cross (2 min); B returns with the torch (3 min); D and F cross (11 min); C returns with the torch (13 min); B and C cross (15 min). 2 Four shoes – three left and one right, or vice versa, and three socks. It doesn't matter how many socks there are to choose from. There are only two colours, so if you have three at least two must match. 3 No. If the woman is a widow, he must be dead. 4 Yes. 5 Not possible.

Chapter 7

Creative test 1 1 You will then be second – you would have been third before you overtook. 2 You can't overtake the last person – there's no-one behind the last. 3 (a) *celebrate* is the only word that expresses a positive action; (b) *demean*, because every other word has an animal in it s**cow**l, depre**cate**, tra**mple**, cele**brate**, demean. 4 A nonagon – a nine-sided shape. Count the number of sides – there are 3.1415. This is the value of pi. The next digit would be 9. 5 There are more Chinese men than there are Japanese. 6 Door number 8. When the foreman said 'first eight doors', the carpenter assumed that the foreman had stopped counting at the last faulty lock. 7 Cut it horizontally through the filling.

Creative test 2 1 There is nothing that says the lines have to be parallel or that a tree cannot be in two or more lines (see diagram). 2 As the yacht will rise with the tide, the water will never get any higher up the ladder. 3 They are two of a set of triplets (or quadruplets, or more). 4 Pour the water down the hole and the ball will float up and out. The bats, net, pen, etc. are distracters – none of these are any use. 5 He notes the time on his friend's clock when he arrives, and again when he leaves, calculating the elapsed time. When he gets back he works out how much time has elapsed on his clock, subtracts the time at his friend's from this and divides the answer by two. That gives him his travelling time. Adding this to the time he left his friend's house gives him the time at which he arrived home.

Creative test 3 1 Zero. It's a hole – the soil has been taken out of it 2 Throw it straight up in the air – unless it's windy, in which case you'll have to work out a suitable angle. 3 They both tell the right time twice a day. The one that gains will do two 12-hour cycles every 12 hours. The one that loses an hour every hour has stopped. 4 Holes in the sides. 5 She was buying house numbers. 6 Tuesday, Thursday, Today and Tomorrow. 7 Pour the juice from glass 2 into glass 5.

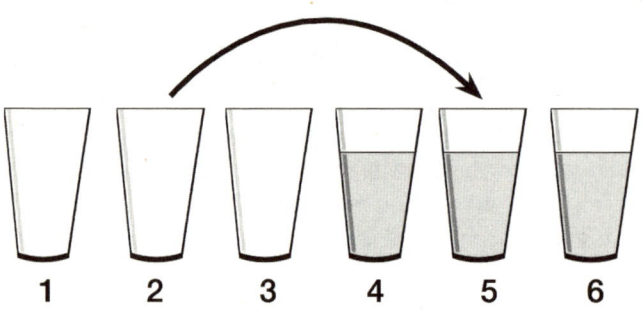

1   2   3   4   5   6

Creative test 4 1 Square covers can fall down the hole if placed diagonally. Round ones cannot fall down any which way. 2 No-one. You give the keys to the man, ask him to take the old lady to hospital and say that you'll collect the car from him later. Then you wait for the bus and renew your relationship with your soulmate . 3 Take one nut off each of the other three wheels and use those to fasten the fourth. 4 Turn one switch on and leave it for a minute. Turn it off and turn the second switch on. Go into the room. You can see which light is controlled by the second switch. Feel the two that are off – the warm one is controlled by the first switch, the cold one by the third. 5 You definitely need to think 'out of the box' on this one! Start from A and draw B, C, D, B.

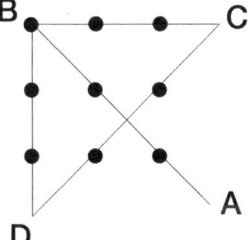

Chapter 8

Warm-ups 1 The bus driver was walking. 2 Let enough air out of the tyres to get under the bridge, then reinflate them. 3 The last boy took the box and an apple. 4 120, because 50 ÷ 1/2 = 50 × 2 = 100. 5 She's not dead. 6 Mary. 7 None. Polar bears live in the arctic; penguins in the Antarctic. 8 The match. 9 Two – 'Will drank *all but two*.' 10 Their left hand. 11 News. The arrows point around the compass, N, E, W, S. 12 If you suspend them both, the magnetic bar will point north. Alternatively, touch the end of one bar to the middle of the other. Magnetism is strongest at the ends of a bar and weakest in the middle.

Einstein's grid puzzle The German keeps fish. Here is the full grid:

Yellow	Blue	Red	Green	White
Norwegian	Dane	Brit	German	Swede
Dunhill	Blends	Pall Mall	Prince	Blue Master
Water	Tea	Milk	Coffee	Beer
Cat	Horse	Bird	Fish	Dog

Grid puzzle 2 Candy has the coffee cake. Mandy's cake is to be delivered to Ealing. Here is the full grid:

Candy	Sandy	Andy	Dandy	Mandy
2	21	10	40	90
Coffee	Chocolate	Vanilla	Strawberry	Banana
White	Brown	Pink	Green	Yellow
Shepperton	Camberwell	Elstree	Pinewood	Ealing

Euler's puzzles The key to these is the number of odd nodes. An odd node is a junction of an odd number of lines. If there are no odd nodes or only two odd nodes, the drawing is possible – as long as you start on one of the odd nodes. Here are possible solutions to numbers 1, 3 and 4. They can all be drawn in other ways. Diagram 2 cannot be drawn.

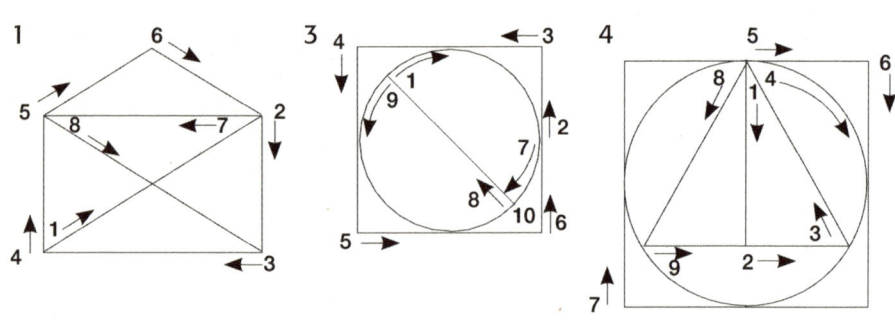

Sam Loyd puzzles 1 Nine hundred people started out in 100 wagons with nine in each. After the first 10 broke down, there were 10 in each. Coming back there were 12 people in each of 75 wagons. 2 As the ride is circular, there are as many kids in front as behind, so you need a number that can be divided by 3 and by 4. Assume 12. One-third is 4, three-quarters is 9, which add up to 13 = 12 + Sammy. 3 It can be done with six arrows: $2 \times 16 + 4 \times 17$. 4 They were a band, not card players. 5 For every $1 bill there are $20 in $2 bills, which gives a unit of $21. $105 is the only multiple of $21 that ends in 5, and is less than $200. So the cashier gives him $5 \times \$1$, $50 \times \$2$ and $19 \times \$5$.